Seguiriyas

Seguiriyas

Ben Meyerson

Black Ocean
Boston · Chicago

Black Ocean
P.O. Box 52030
Boston, MA 02205
blackocean.org

Cover Design by Janaka Stucky | janakastucky.com
Cover Image: Hidalgo, Patricio. Untitled from the series
DE LO FLAMENCO. 2022, ink and acrylic on paper.
Book Design by Anuj Mathur

ISBN: 9781939568731

Library of Congress Control Number: 2023938189

FIRST EDITION
Printed in Canada

Author's Note

The title Seguiriyas is derived from the flamenco palo (or "song form") of the same name. The seguiriya pertains to a sub-category of palos that are united by their status as "cante jondo" (or "deep song"), a designation that refers to flamenco forms whose roots can be traced directly back to the Gitanos (the Romani population) of Andalusia. Despite possessing such an origin, however, the name "seguiriyas" (rendered alternately as "siguiriyas," or "seguidilla gitana") is a corruption of the word "seguidilla," which is a relatively unrelated Castilian and Andalusian folk dance. Both terms contain the verb "seguir" as their root: "to follow." The seguiriyas palo is known to draw on solemn subject matter— poverty, displacement, incarceration, mistreatment, and lost love are among the most commonly recurring themes across the extant collection of traditional lyrics, which have emerged out of the historical memory, social life and material conditions of the Gitano community in the Iberian Peninsula. Though the vast majority of flamenco's oldest lyrics within palos such as the seguiriya and the soleá (another fundamental song form in the tradition) can only be dated back to the eighteenth and nineteenth centuries, they often showcase an awareness of events in Andalusia that occurred centuries prior, detailing aestheticized interactions with Muslims and Moriscos, who were formally expelled from Spain in 1609, making reference to the historical presence of Jews, who were expelled in 1492, and alluding to the heavily discriminatory policies that the central authorities imposed against the Gitano population between 1499 and 1783, which led to waves of incarceration and the forcible conscription of many Gitano men as rowers in the galleys that carried out the state's imperial affairs. As a concept, then, "seguiriyas" presents a recombinant space in which a variegated history wells up and asserts itself on multiple strata of experience: as memory, as a textured voice expressing its grievance, as a body in song, as a lurching melisma that restructures the cadenced impact of sensory stimuli, and as an attenuated tone whose extension reinterprets the arrangement of spatiotemporal spans as they elapse in us. It offers up a form according to which we might internalize, embody and excavate solidarity on an ontological scale: when the voice strains and latches open, we might follow one another through the rupture, together even as we never cease to reside in our own particularity, and time might return to us.

CONTENTS

III.

IV.

Seguiriyas is dedicated to my mother Jill Ross, who brought poetry to me for the first time and has been there along with it each time since – for her bravery, the effervescence of her insight, and the stories she told me when I was small.

Close

Hours sound in me only as the chunter
of rapids.

Each day trails its tassels in my current
and passes.

I.

A sponge,
suffering because it cannot saturate itself, a river
suffering because reflections of clouds and trees
are not clouds and trees.
–Czesław Miłosz

The ellipse of a cry
echoes from mountain
to mountain.

[...]

Like the bow of a viola
the cry vibrates long strings
of wind.
—Federico García Lorca

Kol Nidre

Even rummaging through my insides to find the heavenly court
from where I stand on firm flagstones below the bimah,
I sway in place, correct for turbulence, drone songs
to corral what has strayed:
an oath pitched into distance,
another year groping for return against the tide—

soil slides and sails beneath our feet.
We are always leaving, even when we stay.

We jam our limbs into any shoal that seems
stable, clutch, ignore
the edges that threaten to cut or the strips
that might dirty our hands—
earth bucks us about as if a sea whose tug
would shuck our houses off their lots
and deaden the beds where our gardens grow,
wrench our keys from their fitted locks
and scrub our towns from the maps
on which they perch like sentinels,
wakeful in their unease.

A brush of tassels along my wrist
from the tallit draped around my neighbor's neck,
my father's halting hum, the congregation's chant
in rags flung up to the rafters—rent,
striving to be whole, to be
repaired: a continent bent beneath
the ocean's weight and frayed by travel,
strata cantillating in a tectonic lurch
toward their kin, whose faces they know
but can no longer trace.

Noon On Philosopher's Walk

Ges l'estornels non s'oblida
Certainly, the starling does not forget
—Marcabru

I

An hour off
for lunch, nursing a night
of melatonin (no sleep): May thaw
and the peep of a starling,
its false tongue bunched up
to warble tales of vigor.
A rift between my listless arms
and the vein of chill that lingers
in midday sun—
I buckle onto the bench
and drift.

II

A sandwich in my lap awaits teeth
like the ear awaits noise—I am a stunned swivel
in the moment's abundance: the cough
of shoes in gravel, twigs clacking on bark, the lag
after rapid pullulation. A jagged waft of traffic
from Bloor, then the flick of air
from a sparrow's wing:
a cup that replenishes itself in
the pulse of things, a raucous voice
that stretches its lie to fit
what it covers—the bridge by the path
hovers at the brink of attention
where the cobbles curl their pattern
into rings and the starling's tattered call
erupts from the surface like a fanged spire or a shoot
from the gum of earth, sweeps me
high up into refinement, ascends from the sprawl
of particulars into a prick of spirit
so that the object's false ghost seems a law
unto itself—on that height,
my eye still cannot reclaim its rougher textures from
the smoothness of fatigue
as it combs the shaded path below
and gathers a hidden language of whorls in the grass,
catalogs their discourse with insistent breeze,
the push-and-pull, the bounded friction
of tree branches along the flecked backs

of buildings, the clamor-and-lull, the senses
shoving one another into new tension:
a dam of leaden eyelids, doused nostrils,
dizzying change and a release—

Tishrei

Fui piedra y perdí mi centro
y me arrojaron al mar,
y a fuerza de tanto tiempo
mi centro vine a encontrar.

I was a stone and I lost my center
and they threw me into the sea,
and in the force of so much time
I've come to find my center once more.
—Traditional flamenco lyric, attributed to La Serneta

My body learned its appetite from the hunger of leaves.
I craned and splayed my veins in midafternoon.

The moon beckoned up a harvest and my roots
came loose. I tumbled. I was a stone.

My fibers snagged on rough terrain
and stretched out as the wind pelted me onward.

I wanted to be a stone. My underside gathered rivermud
until the current dislodged me and gnawed at my stem.

I washed ashore. My stretched filaments dried,
grew hard and taut. I was a stone.

I knew no time save that of the moon's shape. It spoke
in a shower of willow shards and date leaves.

The moon appeared to me as if the wrinkled rind of a citron,
and I was uprooted, a sprig of myrtle plucked from the high places.

I was a stone and I lost my center: time stretched me taut.
I bore the marks of my journey. I do not recall where I rested.

The moon is in me like a cold plectrum. It strums my fibers—
they voice the distances. They vibrate from where they are snagged.

Living Together

I locate myself in fits of abandonment
over and over
from/in/among you—imagine
a single cobble scuffed by multiple crowds,
the scale of its transformation:
from bullion to tarnished relic, flesh
to scattered dirt, river to riverbed, stone
to stone.

To move when everything else is moving
is to indulge and over-indulge
the borders of any set/plane/coordinate,
to outrun, to extract volition only as a deserter:
you sat by me and found dawn in night, motion
in stasis, time in my hurry and yours
in my own.

I recall in moments—used up, repurposed
and ventriloquized, parsed and over-parsed into
a horrible manifold/nullity/trace
where love slows and becomes geology:
the antiphon of bone on bone, tree
on tree, cliff on sea and sun
on ozone.

Together we are a surface ripe for invasion,
a telluric slant touched and over-touched
upon which others stagger/stumble/recover,
a clavicle cascading along with the swallow:
vibrant air and the musk of bodies, river
and riverbed, mine and yours, alone
and alone.

Lips (A Retrospective)

I am settled into the nearness of night, brushed
by the bright-tongued glow of the bulb
in the stairwell below me.

A moment's floor can drop out.
The mind can spiral, return:

time makes things large and makes them small,
a falcon that swells in its speed
to dwarf the world's surface with spread
talons and then recedes,
wheels back out on deadened wings to glide, a speck
that circles the eye—

I am alone, but I am thinking of particular words
from lips forming shapes in
particular rooms, how in listening
I would lean forward and the words
would not grow as much as the lips,
and the shapes they made would act out versions of distance
as plosives and diphthongs widened
into a resonant landscape to welcome
the syllables home.

I am watching time, taking measurements
in the separation of seas and seaward skin,
in manes of dust swept down dirt roads,
in the slow climb of night and whatever exchange there is
between its warm weight and the dent my body leaves—
the diameter of this flesh, flushed with noise,
folded in its choir of travel and repose.

Night brims with our gods and their unwritten bodies,
their mighty hands and outstretched arms;
if time had an arm, then eternity would be
the softest vivisection, a talon so sharp
that it is never felt until color starts to leak
and we turn to behold the great bird,
learning of death as we witness
all the distances from it.

Al Cante

If still it is not revealed—

wait.

Voice will fill you, find you
as it finds us all,
with a body for its binding,
the arid thrill of throat and stomach
and each vulnerable patch of skin—

it will make you its rill, a font
for what is not yours.

We cry the discord of our guts:
the squabbling of microbes,
the crossing of thresholds,
the malaise of land
as it turns over from hand to hand—
expulsion, erasure, regeneration.
Resonance brims up and breaches the lips,
the burnt purr of a gullet liquefied by centuries—
blunted nausea set to discover the blade of its instant,
a pointed flake of light, a way
of being hurt by water:

lo jondo. Depths that only
deepen. The shore of a lake
unsettled, in want of longhouses,
caked in scales of enforced glass and cement,
horned with twisted steel.

A fortress on the hill, bereft
of its builder. A cry that is not pain
but runs alongside it: an oar in the arm that pulls
from aboard the galley,
a rush of acrid heat from the stake
at which the punished body burns—
and still a desire to return, an urge
for harvest and new bread to break—

wait.

A cry that funnels errant air into time
and time
and time:

breath will heave its own elegy
and keep on breathing, revisit
every step as one, lengthen when the climb
is steep—it lifts
and is lifted. It insists on coming home
to its children, even so.

It is a stone.

It is the light on a stone.

Its approach is all at once an exit,
a pulse that assembles each instant
by pulling it apart;

it is the throb of motion within stillness,
a figure both lodged in loam and borne away—

and in it we arise, ascend
unquenched, torn, afloat in torn-ness,
heedless and full of desire.

To live is to be buoyed
without knowledge of the buoyancy:

a cry that gives and refuses to give.

A cry that accompanies the cry.

Under the Antigua Iglesia de San Miguel in Guadix

I am a gem of sweat leaning into the lower wall
    where the stonework is smooth around
        the door's frayed wood
    and my skeleton slants unfinished into warmth
the laboring stem of a plant half
    in bloom but deprived of water
downhill   from the old Alcazaba   swaying
    in the age-smooth streets
    at the place where one collides with another
caught in an exchange
    two worlds unable to look
        too mired   to twist free.

Unease in the gaps: each brick is deaf to its brother.

    The tower is roofed in coppery clay
risen amid the bed of a mosque   and formed
    to the tune of its ghost
    made unresolved in its image:
        the father's hand still laced with
    the mother's   hardened one to another
        voices too known   too close
a jewel of presence mashed together in the diaphragm to halt
        such distant architecture
        such building to blot out the other
    and below it   I am a shard of sweat learning

new edges at each node of contact
where hands   have pounded the mortar
where trowels   have dug out the foundation
      where the clefts between turrets deepen
anytime a rift   seeks to nestle down   to linger
and over it   I   am a fly's wing crystalized in sap
      swept up   in the brightening pang—

it is a pressure exceeding touch
a pearl of impact between one and another
      as if a shard of sun has   limned
that old bit of stone poking   bald through a flaw
      in the masonry and the world has tumbled
            end to end like a scroll   wordless but
      in the frequency of a lament: a mumbled dictation
            of bodies sharing nearness in
                  the slippage that their ache enfolds
the rote stumble over   uneven cobbles   the attempt
            to salvage a sealed parade of time
      even as it hobbles in its pomp along the rim
            of a far-flung horizon
            its mass   swung
            from collision to collision
            until I look away   and it ruptures
      and raising my eyes   I find it all
            unbearably near   too close
as if any swath of space remaining between the self
      and what it might once have been
is too exhausted to maintain its dimensions

has collapsed
has been reduced to the buzz
of warm moisture in the eardrum—

so the stones perspire a pressed   pearl of radiance
send it rolling
off that Mudéjar tower atop the unfinished
chapel and the glint   grows itself
along the minaret's echo like   a femur fusing
round a familiar splint to take the shape   of a new chapel
in which the body comes alive with a squint into the glare
finds shelter and a fluttering of form against
the slow dissolution   of hours   and years
and the impact with other bodies
in the soft sprawl of their damage:

as if the gutted building's erosion
might for a moment stand in for the fading
of the flesh's lone abutted tract;
as if in such a moment
there might only be the brow   drenched by coins of sweat
the sun strung in beads across warm hair
the impact between one   and another
the distance that erupts from inside the closeness
the pearl   that erupts from what enfolds it
the hour   coming to collect its tithe
but not yet arrived
not yet sealed in the stones and   up the hill
another car sweeps by.

Summer Storm

The humidity snaps. I would have felt
less wilted in the heavy air
than in the clammy cool of its undoing.
My mother's hair is frizzed and her temple
throbs—she can tell what is coming.
We do not know the road until it is submerged—
raindrift in tildes on the unenunciated asphalt:
a sheeted syllable, its slope a hiss
of current set to hoarsen the drains.

We are in the yard and on the front porch,
nested in red brick and firm wooden fences
when the clouds come in and
wring out torrents, as if the water
is what they are forgetting—
we look down as dirt springs aside
to make way for the droplets
and in the wet hewing stutter we are reminded:

all this time, and the tongue falters in exile—

we speak of home, but really we mean a shape.

The house is carved up by our indent;
the body is a divot of the house's making—

we form and it forms. Our speech
is the rain on its rooftiles and the gale in its shutters—

we breathe and regurgitate:

an axel of air hinges the mandible
so that it flaps and clatters,
finding syllables as if by echolocation.

We look up and all of it seems strange,
a raindrop to be tested on the tongue:
a failure of sight; signs exploded
by the material of their own content.

We find a shape only when what it harbors
is swept away or drowned.

Space collapses.
Menace reinscribes intent wherever it appears—
I say *I meant it to be that way*
or *I never set out to hurt you.*

The basement is breached—
it salivates, does not speak.
The carpet wears a sodden blush
and moisture finds
all the junk fastened
to untended corners where dust
once gathered.

We rush indoors and pat our heads
with towels. Frenetic action. Buckets.
Dismay in my mother's voice.

I have done my best to seal up the windows—
my hands have acquainted themselves with each edge
and plane of the wall.

The house makes itself known as the sum
of its contours—the threat of damage reveals it.

A moment of exile binds the tongue:
words flee their referents
and take on the shape of their own intention.

The will to have becomes the will to remember:

voice times itself as a choral numerology
in which each variable insists
on the truth of its own slice of history and conceals
its motive, immune to inquest—
a grunt, a squall or a whistle lifted
up to surety in the votive cavern,
cased in sleek armor, chiming
then fading in a hurry,
flooding and dwindling—

dying so that it is never to die, saying
I meant it to be that way.
I never set out to hurt you.

Gefilte Fish

                An aside
in the other language   amid the scrape
     of forks:
            a mutter
     a tug between cadences
sharp on my grandmother's lips
        and still slurred in my ears—
I must think of the tongue as a carp
     poached and ground up
         beet-pink
wriggling from shore   to shore.

A heater is dialed
        too high in the den while   the other language
     flakes forth in absent
        morsels:
a familiar taste that my palate cannot index
     a flagging desire never slaked
         or whole in itself   an alloy
     breaking in the briny   lag
leftover when we have gone
        but not been washed away—

the carp-tongue stirs its parts
    reconstitutes
        poises to be bitten now that the teeth
reserve an extra beat to recognize its shape
    and its every noise is an unknown skin offset
        from the birthed body
pulled an inch farther with each elocution until
        it brittles
    disintegrates   cannot
        be felt in full
but descends in tremoring flecks   that lull
    into the fabric   of spent
        couch cushions
    penned in   by loose threads:

glimmered velleities that rend
    memory's collective spirit
and upend the prior mouth's closure over
    any movement of
        the minced tongue
whose length has been   remade
        in the faulty image
of what it once was but can be no more

        pounded
            rolled
    sliced

a fish that no longer resembles a fish
a shore that is no longer a shore.

Considerations

Rain falls in real time, and rain fell through the night—
no dress rehearsal: this is our life
    —The Tragically Hip

Wan afternoon away from home
and the browser window moves
in netted blinks: we all know
he is on the brink—
and then that he is beyond it:
we will no longer
be whetted on his stone,
and his trail will only ever
be a trail.

We crowd onto a strait
of vexed colloquy, step
with care, the blades of our feet
severing fallen leaves even so—
but he is still singing,
northern Ontario red-shifted into
his throat so we can see it at night
like a distended constellation, clawed
into tundra aphorism:
the rake of salted January gravel under
tires, powdered by machine-rust
and frost rinds winding to a crust along
the path, the baritone snap of boots

on morning snow just outside the house
between trees that brandish thin limbs
above the slumbering car out back—

such curious contrariety to find a landscape
in the sounds that seek to cure the land
of its trouble, as if we are shirking one common fate
to claim another—

things get stuck.

We stumble upon the loneliness
of particularity, each of us
by ourselves—

we do it together, permit
a sonority that wears in along with our joints,
commits itself to trespassed wax and redirects
our disparate syntax into the sprawl
of its own time:

a languid night of rain,
the sprint through yet another decade of fixity,
how the distances that we must traverse
in order to run away or come together
are so cavernous that their echo can form a melody,
that for an hour of the same languid night
we can listen in real time and
in their condensation and their downpour
we might discover our own lives.

Scenario: Entry

I

The river just beyond   where
        summer fires have weakened the slopes:
        debris has bulged
                to the outer lip of the bank
        we are stopped
something happens with gravity—
hands brush the edge of numbness
        light
settles on greyscale
        does not change.

In frail shade   at rest
        pale sun webs   through foliage
mottles skin
        daubs the moss ahead and the moss
                behind—
        the patterns wind along swells of
                breeze and in
        the deepening of hours   a caw
                from among the trees
        carnage
                of a rodent breaching its bush
        a vulture's loping gait   above like
                the languorous swoop
        of a minute hand on its path.

By the river refusing time
          until
hue drains from the world around us—
          we squat on heedless stones   over
the water   watch feldspar dampen to phlegm
          peer
                    into the copse of pines
whose trunks are ashen spars
          whose needles
are smudged together like rubbed charcoal:
          oneiric spires that dissolve into dim sky
                    humming with the cold
          of other seasons—
no salve for the desire   no sap
          to trap what runs away.

When night arrives our eyes must adjust
          to loss: we must squint
for the warmth of bodies—
          they respond
                    they make a music
                              we do not know it.

By night there are threnodies
that sound from corded throats
          but snag on the gums and
pinch off in glottal wisps—
the dumb brush of symphonic palms on thighs
          dragged skin   to haul

a dawn ictus from the tar of time
and so   to set things into motion:
flowers stretch until their pollen wicks rust
        and curl as   their stems pool like
                wax into earth then
        new seeds spawn   thickening with age—

all we feel are petals on our chthonic tongues
        though the taste
is of chalk and wet grit lapped from the river
whose current is greyed by silt
        whose path is clamorous
                with summer
        and nameless detritus;

all we hear are hours and days
tickling our nostrils like ragweed
at the tangled border of an endless field
        compressing pollen to wax in our ears—
and then some chatter from underwater
        from the bedded stones and the pine droppings
                some mute chorus
        scraping us into light.

II

On the new day
          rapids effervesce in me
     headlong amid organs
untrussed
     fanned to a rush—

pores fulminate and slacken

          history
     mulls in sinew:

land is knotted around me
     hunched
     incommensurate
my body is midden-weight atop its pallor
          muscles bunched
     to trace the lag of air
skinward follicles skittering ajar in the murmur
     atria unlaced into a hacked calm.

A colossal illumination
          will helm
     this new body into which I
          dawn
parsed in implicate glow
          drawn
like water from the well

            slow   then
streaming from form   to form—

I am raised and razed back into a subject
    dune-dry
    rustling with current;

I am a cartridge for unextended light:
    the moisture beneath baked sand
    a vernal relic petrified in the glacier.

In rivulets
    days drip and carve runnels
runnels widen
            to tributaries—
    the particles skip and rush in herds
conduct sun in flecks with
the slip and sprint of their haunches
            gait uneven
slabbed flanks that glint as they brim and surge against
    the pasture that enfolds them
            the bells round their necks
    sounding daybreak and dusk through
            the parched beaks of birds:
        they drift   on familiar paths
their current rattles the sturdy wooden fence—
        chattel twisting   in brusque rebellion
            then   shambling on its way.

We all move
        to where we are going:

the body wakes into its husk
    sleeps
        rouses
    slips between—

away from me
    a crane's whoop hammers still water
where the river gives way
        to wetland;

each sun falls on the heart
    like a hollow tire
        slapping cement.

Speaking of Fountains

In memory of Khalid Esmail

Hours do steady things to the crevice
of a syllable, scrape out its trough then
elongate its release into arable clay:
a crease in which we collate years and
age softly, mingling when the growth abates.

I am thinking about this as I listen
to a fountain, which is the longest phoneme,
a dream of the universe blasting dark matter
to project our souls onto canvas beyond
the flecked stars: water outlasts history,
and takes us with it when it goes—buildings
climb tall and decline like chipped quartz
in an exemplary cave, gleam and
don coarse tunics of loam.

Lives tumble like stones into a pool.

No thirst is ever alone:

speak to me and imagine a fountain,
tongue always clutching a corner of the word,
always touching the reply. Imagine centuries
in wry ripples when a sentence falls
to stipple the surface of the water,

then think of your lips as loose quartz
clattering damp together in
the sun-slick mouth of a cave,
where minarets and steeples rise
and the song of the body's nearness
is that of its going away.

II.

What little there is beyond impermanence
conspires with a half a mind on the original
to sew us closed
—**Liz Howard**

The openness of a face which has not yet been sculpted. The
bloom that comes of flowing to the depths of what nourishes
it again and again. Not a mask given or attributed once
and for all, but an efflorescence that detaches itself from
its immersion and absorption in the night's most secret
place. Not without sparkling. The light that shines there is
different from the one that makes distinctions and separates
too neatly.
—**Luce Irigaray**

Scenario: Reprise

I

Bad guitar by the river   and dogs
     jawing through the shallows panting
          as puddles gust their paws:
     they hurtle
their sides graze bushes that billow where
     flowers split
          the listless water:
     yellow on our shoes
          yellow in the dirt we sit in—

     on the opposite bank there is singing
and the plucked strings barely   prick
     our ears against
          the splash of the dogs
     the muted laughter
the sting   of all this inarticulate light.

On the street above the old wall
          that runs with the river   the whooping
               of children   slick bulerías
by the cafés in   the droop of their awnings   the clink
of coins   the thud of the crowds—
          they do not see us below them:
we crouch   by the bridge where foliage shrouds

the stone   where the bats
            pelt out from their holes   plunge
    by narrowing glow and halo the dogs in
            their rictus of water
as dusk's glare grows   and we gloam in our limbs up
        through our listing brows   and our spines that grasp
            the twisted curve of the bank.

        We gesture
    wrists firm   hands
    heavy as tired birds alighting
            our bodies filled and drained:
decanters for the dipping sky that darkens   down
            into the stream below us—
another abundance to ford   another glut
        to succor this earth into which
            the hours sow us.

Beneath the balconies by   the back end
        of the church where the river
        chokes to a rill   dusk spills along
        the thinning trickle into stillness—
the constriction of a throat
        hilted   with warm air;
                the way silt
        noses between the roots of brittle weeds
in wait of a better season:

things move
in place—
forms
pour into themselves.

Tissue exhausts its stores in the mind
courses in step with
the eye:
the adhesion of forehead and
breezeless hair   the suck
when chatter elides along
the braid of current
and twining guitars slide off
the plaited cascade then
lose their way—

cacophony lifts   sutures into calm;
the hour widens;
our gaze swoops in a new time:

above us
swifts glide
to Africa on pendulous wings.

II

A whirl of hue in
　　　the river where the bush casts a shadow
on the maze of ripples:　　　it looms
　　　a dazed ziggurat atop　　　the water's rush
　　　a vast dark bloom beckoning the other bank
cold　　　but nothing to shiver at—　　　a flush
　　　in the arms　　　and not the torso
the pungent blur　　　of skin in the moment:
　　　warm fur　　　cheap tobacco
　　　　　and wet.

　　　In front of us the dogs
　　　　　have rattled their coats—
　　　their muscles slur
droplets tattoo the earth where they stand and then
　　　　　they curl
　　　like raucous streamers
　　　　　bucked by breeze:
　　　in me a mind subverts its ease and unfurls
a dim tone shredded　　　into a howl
a spray of round stones that the river sews
　　　mid-flow to its gesture
　　　bankless　　　undulant
set to scrape loose whatever
　　　is bedded under it　　　a hand
　　　　　sweeping crumbs to where
　　　they have been made to go—

we know now to draw the water in buckets
    in skins
        lekabets galuyoteinu
    to hold from inside the scatter
to gather in what once grew—

the stream still streams
    the dogs give chase   together   locked
        in a sinewy ellipse
    they
            ask:

there is no question on their lips.

Water goes
    noise goes   light
        goes and new light comes:

a year like crumbs in the current

    a drought
        a rain

the river tipped from its own spout
    the body idle
        forming to the pour

moving how water arrives in us

coming and coming and never coming back.

Granada After the Correlation

In the least measurable world, mind
squalls in a shred of swamp, recuses
each pearled dreg, nips at its own heels—
but moves, refuses walls, pretends
not to know nature even as morning shifts
docile in its stall and huffs
to its own ends: a crick
in the aubade, waking up stiff,
tongue all stuffed into a calligram,
knotted with sweetness and bile—
it is thus that the measureless day
imprints itself, bray
onticology or hyper-object all you like.

A wealth of speedbumps on our way
to mortifying the surface of dazzling change—
pity the mind, rattling on and on
with a bog-moon above to fortify
its dim aegis: we prod it silent
not a moment too soon.

I am in the clasp of a different morning,
where sun begins to seep through every slit
in the closed door and the houses outside
are impregnated with flowers—
you can smell it from the streets and

the terrace bordering the other room,
where threadbare towels dry on the line
and dogs sigh in the dizzying heat.

We do it like this: we insert the subject
into an impossible image and watch
it yearn, watch its ears prick, the faint burns
where air meets its skin—we tell it
that it is a mind; we ask it for nothing.
We wonder what it can see.

Warm air pierces the curtains, sweetens
my nostrils with gusts of plant slough
flung in estuaries against a dam of attention—

I have already felt the breath burst from
your nose as you pace the garden
outside my window.

You hum to yourself.

I can hear your lashes
like gummed cicada wings in the waning dark.

Daybreak Translation

Hay que avanzar, hay que avanzar

We must move forward, we must continue on
—Javier Egea

*

Take dawn and make it a hinge,
as if night is a shutter to be tugged
up or down
in the talons of a rock dove, pulled
from above, where the pulsation of wingtips
warps air into pillars banished sharp
against the empyrean cliff, whose summit
is a vertex in the fold
of a face averting.

Whatever might become an aubade
is sealed in the dove
as it curtains the leavening horizon:

the watch fires soften as night recedes,
and a restless mind might leave as the bird leaves,
laden with unthought trills to greet
a dawn that is already stolen.

Whatever is in the dove
is not coming out—
the light does its work:
beacons do not illuminate,
faces are too clearly seen.

*

Dawn is not a span in itself, only the town—
a thermometer
whose mercury climbs when it bathes
in the heat of a fever: a combustion
of night, an alchemy.

We ascend to sentiment through dusky earth,
frantic as moles, squinting before
the tongue of dawn,
which is a vertical flame drawn around the wrapped
wick of our bodies, skimming off stray cells
to capture translucency beneath
the fragrant drape of its smoke.

Waking siphons fluid from the fullness of the dream,
in which we are visited by warmth
and then the mad enunciation of touch—

we stutter and stutter,
burn one another and are burned by day,
and so retreat to plumb the fecundity
of soil, craving doves:

we will rise trowel-clawed and paralyzed with light,
borders unexplored,
dislocated same as a voice in the dark.

I am sifting the embers while we wait out dusk's imprint
and pour the greying stuff of selfhood into other vessels
amid the mole-blind inversion of morning—
a distillation of dreamt vigor, idle until
flame becomes world and so
can no longer be a flame:

daylight is when we can see through the barriers between
flesh and the fire that warms it, when sight
dissolves all shapes into
the incompleteness of your skin.

Particles billow then in formless effusion
along my lanterned tongue
and I cannot find the houses or the doors
or whatever is different in you—
we are in want of a vessel to hold the exhalation,
in want of a proper vowel; we live
only in a language of touching.

Daylight is a span and not the town,
a warmth stretched over the hand's motion,
like if you drew my anatomy as it is seen:

exact lines imposed over the lens of nothing, unable
to feel its edges until you trace them.

*

Night is like a knife when it bucks our clasp,
grasped too loose as it slips
from the orange I am slicing and
clatters onto the counter.

My hands are too wet and too sticky—
I don't know how to ask anything to stay.

Put your ear to the hide of the subsiding dark,
hear its organs thrum and clot with heat:

Look—I am slicing fruit for you,
picking at its thick cold skin, and night
is peeled, pressed until its insides are
a translucent gasp on the horizon,
light a spattered burst of sugar and acid.

Citrus billows over the opposite hill,
opens like a petal in my nostrils.

I do not know how to ask anything to stay.

*

The gravity of remote stars disfigures us.

In the alleyways webbed around the house, we are pulled apart
into lofted cries that disturb
still-sleeping ears—

our shapes are flung and pitched;
our shadows lengthen and contract:
the flickered movement
of a tongue as it brightens with words—
the staccato palings of dawn as it stirs.

In its fullness, light severs us from
the firmament's tug—an occultation:
to cover the great bowl in which
our particles are mixed, to let it all harden
so that our anatomy swirls back
from vaporous dark and
dissolution—
we regain ourselves in amassed tissue;
the arteries rush and hum,
and in my body there remains a relic
of whatever penumbral air it was
that hooded your eye at dusk.

With the maker's stolid arrogance, daybreak
refuses to put us back together
exactly how we came—
we entangle ourselves in the celestial fabric
of what has been taken from us,
bundled into the house, eyelids
stiff with the crust of sleep,
fluttering until the lit world takes form.

You will not recognize us once the dawns
pile up, once our bodies depart
from the station where they are stalled
and return with insides stained
by clouded coal, with soot darkening our eyes,
to look again upon the sharp-boned throng
of buildings as they nuzzle at the sun.

Workers begin to pace the walkways of the city,
engines cough, and pavement hefts their weight
on sighing shoulders.

Seasons are demolished into impressions
that discolor old stone.

I do not know what marvels
we are paving over with all this light;

I do not know who is pressed from
the stony shadow of recall,
what intimate dialect we erase.

In the indent of this month I will feel your touch
amid the scuff of multitudes:

this sullied city of the heart
unravels its crowds,
coils them in tinted trails
through deposits of rubble—

we become ripe juice suffusing
a dumpster's trove,

dye forking paths
through stacked cloth,

ore
veining the bright riverbed.

Cantabria

THE FEVE TO CABEZÓN DE LA SAL

Every day it is the same:

the train sways ungainly on its track,
the hills hurtle by, the cattle graze,
the gray river shrugs up a froth—

the remainder skimmed off from our lives is stone slag,
the grit that breaks loose
in their collisions with history.

My head lolls forward onto the window,
a reflection that looks beyond itself,
a body in motion that does not stir—

alluvium gathers from the river, layer upon
layer plastered up into hillocks that bulge
one atop another like piled entrails
crushed into the shelf of a rib:

heaped dispersion. Enlacement:
each instant of brightness clings in itself
to find a name for its opposite—
days are deposited into what they once were.
All water is what it erodes.

THE ROAD ABOVE CARMONA

Every year it is the same:

a lone car purrs by on the thin band of asphalt,
rains pound the dirt into mud,
the cattle graze, the slopes froth slick with dew—

the villagers carve spiked wooden clogs each winter and tramp
door to door through the mire: the remainder is a house,
its rooms filled and emptied out in the collusions of history.

Young people set out first for the larger towns, then the cities.
The stones that sheltered them remain where they are stacked,
bodies that stir but are not in motion—

lives extract themselves in deposits
like alluvium hewn from its valley at the river's passing,
dispersed by years of wind and rain
until they flare up into cowslip, thick grass and sky:

an entanglement of limits. Unified departure:
each balconied house adheres to its centuries,
grows dense in its compression between the hills.
Valleys open into that which they do not contain—
all erosion is where the water went.

A Study of Acheulean Tools

In winter the hedges clatter like bulrushes in a gale,
hammering on brick—
a stutter, a rasp,
the pop and singe of air.

I want to learn a brumal friction:
the brittle scratch
of leafless bushes along the walls they rest on,
the strike of flint once the season
scrapes into its furrow,
a cold spark darting aside upon contact,
licking and fading.

To be seared by its ridged tongue
is to be thrust into history:

time chips flakes from us until there is a blade,
a grooved edge in place of the cortex,
a pocked grip by which
we are wielded.

Bare twigs whip and snap against the brick
and we speak over gusts of wind,
knapping our noise against the larger clamor
until it is a nodule pounded to a frangible tip—

we are clasped in a hand,
biface and fully honed, sawing
through fabric to fashion clothes,
severing gristle from
hacked bone, driven
into wood to call forth its sap,
reshaped, reworked, and gripped anew:

sharp then blunt, then sharp again,
we wear each slight indentation of our work
like a new disguise
that might alter our unchanging core.

Tekiah Gedolah

Wind through the ram's horn. Bone-stench,
a blast from the varicose canal. Stillness
slants the swaying crowd—I await the lengthened
tone even once it spills into my ears:
the breath is sapped of air before it ever fills,
stretched and pale to be preserved, dead but not—
time is a leech that lets the note like blood,
a year milked out into the swollen abdomen of history,
its woolen pulse that ebbs from organs out to breath
and back, our corner of Toronto in a holding pattern
of sleek cars, finery, forgetting. Blithe assurance
that we are special. Wind through the horn.
The call, a muscle wrenched beyond
its axis of return. Time is a leech.

Durian Sunday

He slices it open and savors its pungent organs.
In celebration he works sparklers into its weathered hide—
the three of us watch them spit their brilliance about.
This is culture.

The sidewalk is a reliquary of voice—
all these vocabularies to mean the same kind of love,
to count out the lychees,
to weigh the musky durian.
The astounding multitude scrabbles for shape,
for a vehicle of differentiation—
storefronts pulsate in neon and trumpet their characters:
dim sum and churrería, bar, bar-grill,
and always the scent of durian
to space out the cacophony.

When we buy it, we know only how it smells.

When he saws it in half,
its innards are bedded
in hive-forms and enmeshed where they rest
side by side, their channels of exchange
disarticulated in the scintillant syllabic fizz of sparks,
and it is as if there are two dialects voiced in unison,
striking one against the other like flint on steel.

We listen in the way we know how:
our ears seek out only the chance
of illumination and carve
a steady swath through everything to find
no noise beyond the sparks, .
which drown out the layered amalgam of their source
as they spray around the picnic table where we are sitting
and light up the lit afternoon.

III.

The event ... in its impassibility and impenetrability, has no present. It rather retreats and advances in two directions at once, being the perpetual object of a double question: what is going to happen? What has just happened? The agonizing aspect of the pure event is that it is always and at the same time something which has just happened and something about to happen; never something which is happening.
—**Gilles Deleuze**

We will have been interarticulate, I believe, in the field where annihilative seeing, generative sounding, and rigorous touching and feeling require an improvisation of and on friendship, a sociality of friendship.
—**Fred Moten**

The City Remembered

Summer when the backdoor rug frays under
the sun's desire, which comes straight in from the yard,
always beaded through the same tree,
plumbing its leaf wall—
a procession of similar days gathers density as
it crawls, multiplies
like the fallen maple whorls strewn
across asphalt in the driveway: ersatz childhoods
that I might have lived, identical cities
that shudder to a halt the instant
their difference comes into relief.

If the streets' chaotic coil begins
to resemble a map, then I
am less apt to be conceived in the form
of what I was—I was a sieve,
I was a phrase uttered

in the deafening minutiae of its own likeness.
To return to the past is to regain
an impossible anatomy, a flesh unfettered
by knowledge of its borders, a view
of Toronto as a nude gargoyle that defies
the order of things: city strutted and
chambered like bones, fish-gutted
and girded by webbing—renegade parts,
cautiously worded to form
a heart. Trucks clatter through its veins,
and beyond the docks a watery diaphragm
flexes to propel breath from its lung.
Every iota of its tissue dances, dissembles, speaks
with a different tongue.

But on my return the chimeric city eyes me
and its torso is the same
as its face—the tall grass quickens
with crickets, the crowds shift in their linens,
and still each lineament is petrified
in a slumber that would be my own,
a rest that is the burden of relief once time
has plundered and hardened—
such ardor for what has passed us by,
for a tension the muscles have since released:
the lame leg that the hour favors
and its mounting disease—
no record of counting to parse
the earth's infernal ease. No sum sufficient
to take me from its crease.

The Toronto Purchase

Every impulse towards self-withdrawal bears the marks of what is negated
—Theodor Adorno

We did and did not choose.

Loose-fitting black shoes chafe my arches
    in the Sanctuary where solemn velvet converges
        with the air's papery snap.

Ribbed rafters.   My head tipped back and lapsed into
    the claustral memory we   have guarded   and then
    the quelled unease that comes   after:
        our newly prosperous repose
whose scrubbed scent   still clings to us when it has wafted
    up into the perfumed height
and a weathered rasp that stows away beneath
    at once lofted   and tamped down—
    a tuneless or wandering hum
    kneaded by time.
    It braids   bakes   leavens into
new laments that cast out all who mourn beyond their walls:
our reverent gall   when we presume to mend the world
    before we countenance
    its depths   or sprawl.
Another stronghold of bereavement into which we have been born:
    a well   where we purify while others parch
    an exile reproduced—

tikkun
      but olam supplied a priori
tucked behind these ramparts of affirmation
      from which we survey the terrain—
and then Toronto   there   beyond
      an unminded mystery for those
who do not drift like our most time-frayed liturgy
      or stray.
Its lure: the urge to find
      and dwell there   with what I
      found on my inexorable march away—
to unbind   to reemerge.

A monadology of the city: the internally coherent house
      whose halls are twined by glittering multitudes
its maze of bricks   raised by permissible hands
      singular   layered into its tenement slew
      razing the sediments beneath until
the mazy store of memory that they secrete
      is gouged   pared down   dispersed—
      a tuneless or wandering hum
that hovers at the far end of every corridor
      the creak of former occupants   sealed up
      by spotless tiles   the walls
      within which they persist
      wrongs done   wrongs unrecalled
      speech in excess   of arbitration.

A hum: the ambit of our flawed
     foundation stone   captured
       denied   and still
     their voices arrive shredded by
each a priori of the city's law   obscured
       by newer noise
     stranded where the brickwork's face
     goes unexposed behind the well-fed plaster
       of contracts   and condominiums—
     my ear ought to have been more poised.

In the Sanctuary we brood on ditches   wire
     furnaces   grim numerology
       our splendid clothes intact
     refusing the world   tract by tract:
olam a priori—   a decision already unmade.
       Only dregs expended in gauze
     the essential scrum of life
into which our entry is delayed   another year
       and this unspooling tourniquet of days.
Difficult for the ear to forget—   still it knows
     a tuneless or wandering hum
lacerations of voice that threaten   to spill:
     respite that never comes
       transfers of land
       purchase and theft
     signatures bereft or marred
and then dislodged into undesignated earth.

The city leavens:
another stronghold set to petrify
its new abridged   eternity in
      roofs enforced   by hardened steel:
      beams   latticework   bayonets—
            purposeless oppressive shard
      windowless monad whose nascent opulence
astounds   and consolidates the disregard.

A Cold Series on Sense

SUB/MERGE

Some moment of breach from the turreted sea—

palisades comb up beyond
                reach   and the whole hulk of land
        discovers depth there   on its own tip
undrowned   the sagittal crest
                of a behemoth bound by hard walls of brine
laureled in panicked birds   amid the soaked   snap
        of underbrush   the lurch
                of larch-addled gale and   scrapped pines:

time is a ripple that finds its shape on the body's shore.

Even when we are in limpid sun   it slides
                off our skin like a deluge   and our feet
        dodge little waves—   *La Grande y Felicísima Armada*;
a shattered prow—   each neural tatter blown branch   to branch
                then the musty burp of the car upholstery
        as it sinks under us   the engine's surge
                breakwaters sparring the dike
        miraculous   dormition:

impact is a sigetic lick
  a formless siege on the nerves   air
cuffing the cheek   wet sticks underfoot—
nec facundia deseret hunc   *nec lucidus ordo*
      only Toronto torn from winter   cased
         in bedraggled slush   eaves
      flush with melt—   a new drowning
         to overcome   a new disappearance.

SUR/FACE

I resolve on the surface of daily comfort—

        not under it   in the depths   but grasping an oar
skin nipped by ripples and   beneath me the mind:
        perhaps a salve   perhaps an entropic snarl grinding
ashore   a clot   blooming in the mens rea.
    I breathe   before the fathoms can batter my throat
            I cleave a porous oratory of   membrane
with greedy mouth to work   the sonority of event and find
        a plane abreast   the chopping wave—

a shape is what the hour washes out of us.

        Even when air runs across our hands
it learns dimension as it comes undone.
        It is already the city   and we are already gaped in sun
our steps molded to slick sidewalks   paths formed
by the same laws   the same lattice of brick and bark—
            it is all sinking in   has sunk
wet on contact   this lossy apparatus
        flooded too soon   drunk on labor:

impact sags the nerves into
 disunity—   madly the swerve of pigeons
           madly the coo of tires—
infelix operis summa, quia ponere totum   *nesciet*
      nothing done   no order complete
            only a planed puddle by the road
      a membrane of frost
           your face   knowing it.

SUB/REPT

Every impression is at first a drowning—

not to be filled   but rather stifled: a hollow thing
        with all entries and exits stoppered   seawall
dislocated from its salt   the sentry smudge of coastal pines
                and no breeze to carry their sap
        vertiginous scales washed up in the wake of fleeing fish
and then this packed mass of reef coiled beneath the skullcap
        getting rinsed   flap after flap of the coral awash
                corridors soiled by spectral algae—

concept is a droplet weighted for dispersion.

Even this breaker of wind   rattling
        the waste bins makes   a peninsula of my skin
runs around and away   lies   reveals itself
        to be a ghost   a trash bag flapping
                on Kensington Avenue   specks of slush
whipped up by the gust of passing cars—   tawdry shock
        a flinch pooling on your brow and   nothing—
a sensory slip   an eschaton toward spring:

impact digs out the interior of   each nerve
        and the mind finds itself outside
scraping through a muck   of salt-soft ice—
        ordinis haec   uirtus erit et uenus.
In brisk air a scarf's seam nudges   nags at the throat.
        Scraps of vertigo: we float   we ebb and pulse
a twig bobs and now   it is sluicing into the sewer's depth—
        an accident   a plenitude in your glance.

SUR/RENDER

There is no history until it encloses the aging of its vessels—

    it inheres in the life of a droplet   whose innards
have learned the slow collapse of velocity   plummeting
below the surface until   dark pressure
    blasts everything from its lungs like   a smith
heaving at the bellows   and all we want is to outlast it
       to ascend rung by rung until we can look down
at the depth that binds us still   and know
    that it is different from us   that it will end:

time is not a ripple until it finds the body.

Even when air seeks out the cheek there is no skin until
it arrives   until we feel the weight   the erosion
    the layers of peeling paint in the alleyway behind
that faulty TD ATM—   manic accumulation sublated into
    a law of swarms   *contra los hombres*
no contra los elementos   a terrible friction to whittle us away
    and keep us warm at night   a tide
      that smothers us before it retracts:

impact is another face etched onto the nerves   a blow
        an embrace—   your brow creases its hours in wave forms
and a new chronicle of flesh comes to roost in   the gaps.
                Pleraque differat et praesens   *in tempus omittat:*
some moment of breach   in which time leaks and laps—
        and we are its disposition   the forking of its path.
I do not know if you know it or if   I am knowing it
        on your behalf but   I hope it is yours.

Niceties

You never asked—

my day went like a civilized pall.

It was the buildings strung out along Yonge Street,
a stretched politeness,
a seam lining the throngs of affluent young lovers,
the businesspeople, the clustered forgotten.

A habit of accumulation, when the longest thoroughfare
sags limp into the lake, poleaxed
by its own empty complexion—a question
of society:

we are the dimple on a grinning void.

Each new block sprouts skyscrapers faster than gossip—

there is an entire recombinant other to be glimpsed
in the brilliant mosaic of mirrors and steel:

imprints. The desultory wraith of another place.

We opt for a cultivated love,
and leave each other alone.

You know me by rote.

Two Months in Granada

I take a walk at midday when even the dogs slacken with sun and
chatter dulls in the squares. I am twisting like hair in the heat
through alleyways and with each turn the Alhambra reappears,
the trees clatter and sway, the old white houses burn to the
touch.

Boabdil rides away from the city in the clearness of winter,
and a thin glare churns off the fortress walls. He stops, blinks—
seasons stream into finitude and learn a new way of moving
forward: squeezed into the sheath of their limit, diverted by
the seal of his departure. He sits like a stone. He awaits a new
buffet of wind, desires to remember his own skin.

So small a thing to be this near to it, a whisk of the eyelid, as
if the beginning of my glance is the end of his: it is the roar of
return threshing my eardrum. On the hill, Boabdil shifts in
his saddle, tightens his shawl against the sharp January cold.
Crowds swelter in the narrow street and displace gingerly for
a fruit-bearing truck. The gruff gush of Andalú cascades from
around the bend. A sparrow near my head bats the world with
the tip of its wing.

A rush.
A shudder.

The cacti nod in time.

The years rattle loose.

The Gap

Time is a hedge that we tend with shears,
a shape that grows
whose dimensions remain constant.

If seen, a fragment of time
is mocárabe, a dome honeycombed
to a tip, which meets
the world at the narrowest edge—
a blade poised to take stock
of the moment onto which it plunges:

the coats of sun that enfold the plaster,
each shaped shadow,
each weighted step to streak the stone;

light as flawed preservative;

the incalculable toll of rains.

JANUARY

Boabdil turns his back on the city.

Songs stir and peel open,
bare their insides less like wounds
than turreted flowers
grown on bushes in rows to line
the pond that fills and echoes his palace.

Absence is a pool full of curled stems
that distort the reflection of what is missing—

seasonal litanies, the diachrony
of identical refrains:
reconquest,
empire,
romances fronterizos that sprout
from vanquished soil with buds
already open, like lips
bearing his name.

It is as if the man has never been:

Boabdil is weeping, in the songs.
Boabdil is tired.

Boabdil is not here—
listen to his sighs in the street.

The Gap's Story

A myth of absence must have emerged
at the sharpest tip of the dome,
where time is too thin for purchase.

The vault reaches its apex,
meets the world and sees its reflection
as if in a span of still water—
wider, contents scattered and wrapped
in a scent or a sound,
the glint of midday light,
the panicked shrapnel
of sparrows from a maze of vines.

JUNE

After another visit to the Alhambra,
I pass through the smaller palace
on my way up the hill,
then pause alongside Mirador de San Nicolás,
which is largely empty.

Afternoon tapers heavy
in perfumed leaves and
the vapors of faint sewage.

Pebbles ripple the waterless pool.

In cafés the birds unspool their calls
and dart from wall-plants like
sparks struck from flint.

The faraway chant of traffic. Voices
in plucked strains.

The glint of something taking its leave.

THE GAP'S VOICE

A mocárabe dome can be sensed
as a manner of gathering ordered phenomena
from their hesitant beginnings—
how sun flits into the socketed ceiling,
the particular lightness of a step or
breath, how spoors of blue paint
still linger on the plaster.

Time is what speech is,
a chord that never unites its tones fully before
the hand falters.

The overtone of absence is mocárabe,
all the wedged lives throat-sung
into their cells along the soaring vault,
stored identically—

it is a circle that conceals
its pointed third dimension.

This is the deep song—
cante jondo: a refusal to reveal the end
of a body's feeling or
the limits of its voice's form—

the upward trench of time's sojourn toward light.

JANUARY

When Boabdil fled the city, he paused
on a promontory and looked down upon
the blushing walls that straddled the hill
and must have thought how the gardens therein
were a promise displaced or a moment moored
in the worm-ready webbing of words.

The branches are ordered like a mind
in the gardens (as I have seen them) —
the way a person folds a thought
as if it is a length of silk awaiting
its maker in the sun-stained chamber
where its threads were spun and woven.

Cante jondo is a ritual of reclamation—
a trajectory, the heart's reification
of absent flesh: some beloved specter
unresolved, flung upward on melodies
in order to make space for its descent.
It is a mirror of mocárabe in this,
tracing the same tapered arc.

In its wake, there is only the hope
of a sharpened attunement, only desire—
to resume the chord's falling away
even after its tones have faded.

Cante jondo does not reveal time
but asks us to trace the sweep of its disclosure,
to follow the peaks and divots of its motion
until the following, too, takes on a form: seguiriyas—
the singer's voice wavers upward
to traverse an ornate dome,
slides away off its slopes,
patters astray
and only then comes to a rest.

So it is that all things cannot fit
into mocárabe's parabolic atmosphere:

a loose rustle of noise must always escape, a life
can chirp through fissures in the lower masonry and wane
in its own time.

On the cliff there is no wind and a clear view
down onto the fortress.

Mirador de San Nicolás is silent
then not.

The two guitarists are playing "Entre dos aguas"
more slowly than the original—
the notes need time to reach
the turrets below, and slivers of sun
stow them away to unload them
on the steps by the garden
where the lips of the fountain
gather and blow them
into the stream.

They trill glass rims of light and
waft, stir atop the polished brass hurtle
of current as it wanders—
but the water's sound is of fanned fingers
liquefying the guitar's wood,
the lingering shade of hedges
to muffle the music like a hood.

Life dangles on the seam
of a noise, wades
into its own stream, remains
for the sound of its names on a tongue,
stirs and persists,
departs and renews.

Furled in its ebb, we are waiting to be revealed.

THE GAP IF WE SEE IT

Light's masquerade is determined
by the object onto which
it settles—the contours of the masque carved out
by its thirst for illumination.

A semblance endures,
a hollow shell of what has been exposed
even after its sound has deserted it.

This is what a fountain is for:
a way to shape the world so that water's expression
becomes a noise which neither stills
nor alters—contained, domed in, time
housed in the vigil of its intonation.

A guitarist's hand
makes the strumming circular,
washes the strings one finger
after another—fat droplets plucking
at clotheslines tautened in exact wind,
so that there is pitch
to govern the bedlam of heavy rain.

In the moment of his departure,
Boabdil must have known the world to be
brittle as a dried flower, stamen a bristle
of Toledo steel and towering pikes—to move
in such a place is to be punctured or to watch
something dear crumble like parched petals
beneath the weight of one's fingers.

It is 1492: the Jews will be gone and Columbus
an ocean away. There is no Nasrid king
to pace the gardens of the Generalife.

They will write how Boabdil is weeping
and forget that if the tears were ever shed,
they were not his,
but a liquid of our making
to wet the petals of a rising chord
and wash away the relic of the former bloom—
the tempered debris of its stems,
its treasured, sharp scent.

THE GAP IF WE SHAPE IT

Cante jondo is a profusion
of the voices that have built
the city, plastered into a vault
of perfect stalactites so that
the recombinant soundwave
lilts along the dips
in the honeycombed prisms as
it ascends to the ceiling's
peak and then pauses
at its breathless height before
the jittering fall.

Always spare noise before the lapse
into silence: the palms
keeping rhythm and
a trill from the lung to trail
the final note, then cascades
of strung nylon biting
into the hands that cut their tension,
no longer making the melody's shape—

the depth of a song is measurable only
across unreachable axes, its accreted form
claiming illicit dimensions in the body,
then claiming the body as its question:

wind shifts in its silks,
a liveried frame that billows daylight
to its berth like a rag swiped along a silenced blade
then pads away on careful feet
once the blade is clean.

Crisp lines and precise vertices enclose us,
but do not announce themselves—

we learn of the shape only after it is broken
and the pieces are strewn about the space
that in its wholeness
it once spanned:

orange trees line the paths in the gardens of the Generalife,
and in the palaces the bushes
are newly tended.

I am in the kitchen with a sandwich and the sculpted dusk.

The rooftops glisten
on the slopes below me and distend
beneath the lope of warm air.

Listen—these things take form
as echoes behind
the needing,
exact breath robed in
stucco walls where the warped
chime receding
falls:
wax-skinned leaves hiss
along a slim jineta-edge
of wind like whetstones as it flutes in
to fan fragrance trimmed
from the gardens so that
loose soil thrums over
stones and twigs sing
stunned off glass to rain on
stretched shingle drums.

Nothing to be done—
whatever is in me has earned its stone.

On the opposite hill, the fortress is russet
and lamplight peals offbeat along its domes.

The world will slide away before the chord,
on the shard-tip of a note.

In Memory of Geoffrey Hill

Averroes, old heathen,
If only you had been right, if Intellect
Itself were absolute law, sufficient grace,
Our lives could be a myth of captivity
Which we might enter: an unpeopled region
Of ever new-fallen snow
—Geoffrey Hill, "Funeral Music"

Because it is the exit of something, memory
defies the truancy of a tongue, melds object
and animus in trellised becoming: it is to suggest
entry and to bar it, how there are no hinges,
but still the hinges make their mordant whine.
Because it is the aloneness that takes
the least measurable toll and
endures longest. Because more can be fixed
than the pinned banner of absence. I am thinking
of Averroes and celestial motion:
same as the planets in their spheres,
a life is not an accident, but an event
concentrically emergent with
the laws of the universe. To arrive
is to be fallen, a chronicle of speech already
in ascent, transgressing its Platonic depth—
lacunae and bloodied light rent from tongue
and firmament; your act of healing:
to refuse history its medicine and bear

the brunt of its dead, living
as lives have elapsed, perhaps
unspooling in their stead.

You dwelled amid a landscape shorn
between the blades of one generation and another,
whittled by latent charisma: an eternal will worn
to isthmus by the certitude of years—
you did not shrug the pressure off.
You walked the fields. You spoke
arduously, and nothing was whole—
only disrupted: unfinished relics wicked off
the gristle of shrub and bramble, the slick leavings
of violence in dry soil. Words have grown wary
in their cohabitation with horror, borne the weight
and sagged into disfigurement, to be stomached only as shards—
the unfixable mass begs for restoration: your chimera,
the mystery in which you rest. I often imagined you
in the skin of an expired icon, essential as
the wrought stone of Mercia and its litter of
ruinous arms—but then the gorse gave up
its blooms above the coarsened dirt, and the buds
hidden on the wall-vines parted their lips
in the inevitable breeze, humming songs
of separation: in the world's wavering,
an overdetermination of the soul within the limits
of its spill—to be doused and still to dig a path
through the slavering muck and morass
of loss so that the path itself

might be lifted in place, or housed.

Elegy redeems itself, demands
a rejoinder: to lug desperate weight
across what is gone, to traverse its compass
and topple off the edge, healing incantations,
scrabbling fists and all. Loath to relent,
the burden drags, stymies the ascent that might sate it
and so inflates the sway of its currency: a countryside
in which the spirit sheds scintillae all over, caught
on snarls in peeling fences, pollinating flowers
and hastening the crop yield. In the distance
there are the faint bleats of children and
the rib-whistle labor of final breath;
tendrils of woodsmoke leap
from the chimneys along with the swept fumes
of history's absolution, wafted up
from the clutter of its charred ingots.
Always the strange, spiced musk of home.
Always a familiar voice in air to halt just before
the greeting. It is a terrible thing to leave.

IV.

Each point has as many chances as all the others; the matter about to take form is in a state of complete internal resonance; what occurs at one point reverberates within all the others, the becoming of each molecule reverberates within all the others at all points and in all directions
—**Gilbert Simondon**

Recursiveness, incantatory insistence, is liturgy and libation, repeated ritual sip, a form of sonic observance aiming to undo the obstruction it reports. It plies memory, compensatory possession, reminiscent regard and regret.
—**Nathaniel Mackey**

Cuando canto a gusto me sabe la boca a sangre
—**Tía Anica la Piriñaca**

Para Tocar

I

They took me up into the hills to make a din
with our instruments and our half-guzzled
bottles, crouched rag-tag in the lit mouth
of a cave, then *abre la puerta niña*
and the city below atremble on the precipice of night,
at once enlarging and falling away—

it is only that we are so endlessly moored
in this slatted carapace cluttered with organs and
who knows what else: a lash
of strange unbidden thirst must coil through us
and tauten like lace, that we strive
for such sounds, and croon in the wake
of all that we are not.

II

First the Jews left Madinat Garnata,
took the keys to their empty houses
and held them close aboard the ships and wagons
that carried them away—
and then the Muslims who lingered
were bathed in the holy fonts or disappeared
into the caves high above the city
to sing the songs that remained to them
in the time that they were given:

huddled in a ring on the crest of those hills,
we can begin to imagine untrammeled desire,
how it pools from nothing to fill the rupture
of distance and films idly
in the suspended multiplicity of non-being,
but we cannot prescind the body
from the desire, and so we go about
stumbling upon evidence—the grooves
worn into a saddle of stone where we sit
by the curtained cavern, the melismatic
tumble of the voice in the shadow just
shy of the candle's lick—and we think
that it must be a subtraction, that it is the body
walling us off from the layered chorus
of who else we might have been or
who else we were,
and that whatever stirs there above and below us

must live only as much as it stings in its joints,
as if the purity of its elocution is in
the clean pitch of its breakage from us, the instant
when we hurl the desire far enough beyond the body
that we know it to be other than what we are,
and it catches, a tarnished flake of silver
burrowed into the dust of another alleyway,
the dirt of another hill,
the crossing of another ocean.

Hadar Rimmon

If God would let me return to Hadar
Rimmon, how pleasant my life would be!

I would drink and sate with the water of the Shenir,
Pure, even when the delightful streams come turbid.
- Abraham Ibn Ezra

Sunk in mud, I have dwelt,
unmoving amid indolent dispensations
of famine and plenty
in this place whose bustle multiplies
like seeds within the borders of their fruit,
clamoring against
the limit of its hide.
The buildings shamble skyward
and the yearning grows—
a cobbled path of home and
away and home-away
that winds between the houses
and spills to the rim
of each roughened stoop,
seeps under the tiles and finds the room
where *I have dwelt in exile.*

Rend your mourning garment,
open it up, peel away its skin. Garb the city
in what remains of its grief, drench its ramparts
with lamb's blood and the juice of crushed grapes—
by dusk it will be a pomegranate in the reddening sun,
split open, a patchwork of pale walls
that shelter nested crimson seeds, lamps, corridors,
coppery roofs. Its roads will harbor a tart edge, but
veer off into new reserves of sugar once your feet
learn where to step: you will find globules
of grime, incense, and illumination,
twisted into trails of sweet and
sour and sour-sweet that dry
into the walls of every house and splatter—
they will stain your *mourning garment,*
and give the Healer what is His.

Leave off me now—maybe I'd spend my days in prosperity,
a turban above me, granting me some shade—
there is life here: on the hill there is a maze
of bone-white albedo, swarming with it.
The Albayzín awaits a hand
to scrape its sweetness away: its thirst
is not yet quenched—it does not know
what it stands to lose. We are each of us
a ruby formed in its interlocking folds:
we have piled up into towers and been packed
into ruddy walls, together and

apart and apart-together—we nip your tongue
with the tartness of our lives. On our heads
we have placed a litany of spires, domes
and open sky: we are all thirsty
in this heat, and we are all in search of shade—
there is *a turban above me; I'd drink still water*
from my well in the cup of deliverance.

After Convivencia

1492//1609

Arise to the harp and the bell,
yearn for spiced wine and pomegranate juice.
Make the gazelle return to my dwelling,
call the century back to its hearth in my chest
and chop it to kindling. Dump its ash
into the flower beds that line
the trail in the garden where we walk together,
plucking lilies, resting
in the dark perfume of orange trees
as the sweat cools on our scalps:
thirst cultivates us,
and so we cultivate the soil. We dwell there,
legs folded under streamlined torsos,
restful beneath the orange trees,
flanked by the lilies and the nards:
the hours stalk us—
they take our fleet hooves, gnaw them off and flee.
We stir, but cannot stand.

Her glance, like a gazelle's,
and my insides a fallow field that she once grazed:
the century pants like a gem in us.
We cannot countenance the wealth we leave
behind us when we go, hefting our deities
and the clothes on our backs—

we will not see her again:
her glance is mine, her scent
is yours, and she
is nowhere.
We carry her wherever she is not – she dwells
but never moves or grows:
we are her ungrazable field, our furrows lapsed
and bitten by her hooves—
we find only the vicissitudes of one
unforgiving god or another, whose hand
buffs a generation's breathing body to a shine
and buries it alive in us, so deep that
we cannot excavate the jewel,
deep as her glance
when dusk reddened her cheek beneath the orange trees.

O dear gazelle! What makes you tarry so?
You must be busy still, picking
lilies and nards in the garden there,
shoulder to shoulder with what you can no longer be.
I hope you are enjoying the scent,
which once clung to the clothes on my back.
I hope your skin is cool beneath the orange trees,
and I hope she is with you,
though she is neither mine nor yours:
we are nowhere
and she is there in the garden with
its coiling streams, atop the domes and turrets,
on the balconies where black swifts perch

amid the long light of July—recall
her glance. Know who you have been:
you are not prey, gazelle,
even if you flee.

Tightly
with the cords of my arms
lest she escape like a gazelle,
I grasp at the air in her wake.
She gusts like a gem in me
and I am no longer where she was—
she is my flawless nowhere. In another life,
we walked the garden together,
and our fields never lay fallow—
I fled, and time stole my hooves,
buried them alive beneath the orange trees
where dusk reddened her cheek:
I cannot stand.
The clothes on my back no longer carry her scent,
and so I cultivate her in my thirst.
I bear her indent. I dwell and yearn.
I am not prey.

Pellizco

The blunt pressure of iron
inside
where it comes out

> The throat's debris: shunted
> shavings and pellets, a spree of dead clay
> wrenched about
> by breath, its gnarled passage
> into time

A metallic
keen, surface unsmoothed

> Lurch of iron summoned to taste
> there,
> beyond where the tongue can soothe

> Places where only water will reach
> or fill:
> cavity,
> crevice,
> duct between there
> and here

A pool that wells up;
the well that contains the pool

Dead clay
effusing in the clatter-throat, over-tilled
until it is thinned and blown

Withered sonority of ore
laid bare beneath the intractable riverbed—
a gum unsewn,
sliced by sound

Water
unsure of its own age, pulled
to a blunted thrum, a hollow stretched flat,
a serrated edge along which
everything goes
and everything returns

Cento

I

Land of our sojourning,
you have eyes enormous as millstones:
certain knowledge of the damage.

If I am a weathervane, then you are the wind
burnt in my body;
I envy the earth,
where there is no movement—

the steps that I take to venture forward bear me back
and now you do not know me:

you parted from my side
without appeal,
buried in air
like a turtledove that wanders the hills,
my rattle
in the sand,
the bells' clamor
in my chest.

II

Land of our sojourning,
how I called to you in full voice,
how you never responded to me.

It is a fistful of pins
to plant seeds without collecting a harvest—

already, the trees bear no fruit.
Already, the winter season has begun:

the bird tires of its nest and
I go about searching,
as if it does not hurt me.

I do not gather up the branches.

The hour has arrived,
the harm into which time gives way:
my palms have measured oceans,
weighed the dust of continents.
I am lost—
my grasses never feel the driving rain,
nor does anyone know their homeland, state
or name:
there are so many of them,
well-hoed and free of weeds,
obliged to wear distinctive marks,

past forgotten for the present—
I pity them.

The water flows bitter from me
before it can speak its hunger—
we receive nothing:
look how we are lost.

III

My soul
whose voice endlessly utters
 —oh river!—through the archway,
come near and
know your own beginning:

arise to the harp and the bell, yearn
for the quenching waters,
so composed and untimely
beneath the ground—

their successors will ever afterward
appear before us

as juniper stains
fines and penalties,
a lost boat,
scattering pearls,
earth on the tongue, spit,
my body when I left.

You must throw the scraps away—
you should not carry their images.

They do not cease to pass by,
amphibious and without borders,
though the bells of forgetting sound their alarm:

disordered birdwings in the mouth,
an appointed place
for those who die wanting.

Seguiriyas

I

Take me here, for I am earthbound.

There is nothing on the inside
that suggests itinerancy or
flight—flesh
is no coward. It knows
only fright and stakes its territory even so,
until it wears out.

Wind yammers between branches and fog
whitens the bay—the water
is tacit tar, lagging. Crags tighten and
sag like tired shoulders against the elements:

bodies forget themselves, age,
recall only where they have never been, as if
caught up in the sheath of a past life.

The only particle
that can compass the volume
of its own grief is dust.

II

Take me away, to here.

Here is a particle that endures
beyond the exhaustion of its intent,
finds a home in singular bodies
and becomes plural as they go forth.

Soil here is scooped pell-mell
to meander the topography of
its displacement. The toil of flowers
is that they mourn the seed when
their petals and roots journey
outward and away from
where they were born:

to be blown apart is to disintegrate,
not to be dispersed—scatter yields recuperation
only in a world without time.

Years turn over into a new hurt.

The bushes churn with birds.

III

Take me here, as if you have never been—

all these foundation stones choke
the land into intensity like tefillin
squeezing an arm, seal this litter of
leather scrap, sanded wood and hair tufts
at a bitter prehensile remove:

it is the soil itself that forecloses return.

Culture resurfaces as a panoptic fossil
bent on its own diffuse trail, sashed in the loop
of its incommensurable degradation:
here, our history is an air pocket
gashing the cache—

a lacuna is an economy
of purgation, in which presence
jettisons time in exchange for
an unrecognizable body, and so
averts annihilation.

Land is the heart's latent currency,
minted only once it is spent.

IV

Take me away from here, to here—

we cannot afford to brood:
if it was all so miserable, we never
would have felt the urge, or stood
in the tatters of deserted homes and
wondered with spry fingertips
along their doorframes' jagged lips.

Yearning is an emergent causality:
our particles track their diffusion
to its source, and find the past to be
a bereft flower regathering its pollen—
we transform. Our strangeness
glowers back at us.

We flourish within new borders.

A reverberation, this thing
we are doing here, together,
probing for a slackness in what was,
extracting its tangy oil:

history is overripe in us,
an olive gone black on the branch—

we find it in soil, in soot, in chipped mortar,
in the labor of cobbles underfoot, and we grind it
to a paste, so that it leaves marks when it slips past us.

Our wrists are streaked by remnants.
Nothing in our grip survives.

V

Take me here, where I already am.

Take my hands, which are dexterous with time,
and my feet, which are sore with it—
here is the soul's dilapidated landscape,
tilled and emptied of its stores,
swilled and spat back out.

I am following—
I will continue on.

To subsist, the soul
is a forager, a planter of seeds:
it only stays afloat,
it only doubts.

It picks fallen vernal olives and grinds them into the arches
of its feet. It does not eat
until the soil has soaked up its fill.

At dawn it wakens and hopes for a better home.
It does not recognize itself, and grieves.

Summer comes
and dries whatever has been left behind:

in the hills and on flat ground,
we walk the trails where ruins of old fires
meet a memory of the sea.

The air is fresh and ancient on our tongues—

we keep on.

Open

Hours sound in me only as the chunter
of rapids.

Each day trails its tassels in my current
and passes

and passes on,
lowing for a still pool,
lowing for a stone,
lowing for a place to stop and rest its head.

A moment does not settle—
it finds a new question to ask, another lack,
an undiscovered track

to follow

[...]

to follow

Cento With Notes On Sources

I

Land of our sojourning,[1]
you have eyes enormous as millstones:[2]
certain knowledge of the damage.[3]

If I am a weathervane, then you are the wind[4]
burnt in my body;[5]
I envy the earth,[6]
where there is no movement—[7]

---

[1] Hasdai ibn Shaprut, (Jewish, 915–970, Jaén, Córdoba), in a letter to Joseph, the King of the Khazars, who had converted to Judaism, trans. Maribel Fierro and Esperanza Alfonso

[2] Demófilo (Antonio Machado y Álvarez), *Cantes Flamencos*, 1881 (Demófilo was an anthropologist who travelled from village to village in Andalusia collecting flamenco lyrics)

[3] Sancho Moncada, *Restauración política de España*, 1619 (accuses the Gitanos – the Romani population of Spain – of uselessness and of causing an inordinate amount of damage), trans. Richard Pym

[4] Demófilo (Antonio Machado y Álvarez), *Cantes Flamencos*

[5] Demófilo (Antonio Machado y Álvarez), *Cantes Flamencos*

[6] Demófilo (Antonio Machado y Álvarez), *Cantes Flamencos*

[7] Demófilo (Antonio Machado y Álvarez), *Cantes Flamencos*

the steps that I take to venture forward bear me back [8]
and now you do not know me:[9]
you parted from my side
without appeal,[10]
buried in air[11]
like a turtledove that wanders the hills,[12]
my rattle
in the sand,[13]
the bells' clamor[14]
in my chest.[15]

---

[8] José María Soto Sebastián Soto Vega 'Tío José de Paula' (Gitano, 1870–1955, Jerez de la Frontera), letra por seguiriyas

[9] Antonio Vargas Fernández 'Frijones' (Gitano, 1846–1917, Jerez de la Frontera), letra por soleares

[10] Manuel Molina (Gitano, 1822–1879, Jerez de la Frontera), letra por seguiriyas

[11] Antonio Murciano (poeta payo, 1929–, Cádiz), letra por peteneras

[12] Enrique Jiménez Fernández 'El Mellizo' (Gitano, 1848–1906, Cádiz), letra por seguiriyas

[13] Curro Albayzín, *Cancionero del Sacromonte*, 1990 (compilation of lyrics typical of Granada's Albaicín and Sacromonte neighborhoods), letra por tangos del camino

[14] Frasco el Colorao (Gitano, 1799–1888, Marchena), letra por seguiriyas

[15] Francisco Moreno Camacho 'la Perla' (Gitano, 1833–1891, according to some sources, Sevilla, Cádiz), letra por seguiriyas

II

Land of our sojourning,[16]
how I called to you in full voice,
how you never responded to me.[17]

It is a fistful of pins[18]
to plant seeds without collecting a harvest—[19]

already, the trees bear no fruit.[20]
Already, the winter season has begun:[21]

the bird tires of its nest and[22]
I go about searching,[23]
as if it does not hurt me.[24]

I do not gather up the branches.[25]

---

[16] Hasdai ibn Shaprut, trans. Maribel Fierro and Esperanza Alfonso

[17] José Enrique Jiménez Espeleta 'El Morcilla' (Gitano, 1877–1929, Cádiz), letra por soleares

[18] Curro Albayzín, Cancionero del Sacromonte, letra por tangos del camino

[19] Curro Albayzín, Cancionero del Sacromonte, letra por tangos del Sacromonte

[20] Curro Albayzín, Cancionero del Sacromonte, letra de Juanillo el Gitano

[21] Nubdhat al-'asr (a chronicle of the Christian conquest of Al-Andalus from a Muslim perspective), anonymous, soon after 1492, trans. L.P. Harvey.

[22] Enrique Jiménez Fernández 'El Mellizo,' letra por soleares

[23] Curro Albayzín, Cancionero del Sacromonte, letra de La Conchilla, the first recorded performance to occur in the Sacromonte

[24] Curro Albayzín, Cancionero del Sacromonte, letra de María la Gazpacha

[25] Demófilo (Antonio Machado y Álvarez), Cantes Flamencos

The hour has arrived,[26]

the harm into which time gives way:[27]

my palms have measured oceans,[28]

weighed the dust of continents.[29]

I am lost—[30]

my grasses never feel the driving rain,[31]

nor does anyone know their homeland, state

or name:[32]

there are so many of them,[33]

well-hoed and free of weeds,[34]

obliged to wear distinctive marks,[35]

past forgotten for the present—[36]

---

[26] Francisco Valencia Soto 'Paco la Luz' (Gitano, 1839–1901, Jerez de la Frontera), letra por seguiriyas

[27] Mercedes Fernández Vargas 'La Serneta' (Gitana, 1840–1912, Jerez de la Frontera), letra por soleares

[28] Judah Leon Abravanel, "Poem To His Son," 1503. Abravanel (Jewish, ca.1460–after 1523, Lisbon, Toledo, Venice) was exiled from the Iberian Peninsula after the Expulsion of 1492, and separated from his son, trans. Raymond P. Scheindlin

[29] Judah Leon Abravanel, "Poem To His Son," trans. Raymond P. Scheindlin

[30] Demófilo (Antonio Machado y Álvarez), *Cantes Flamencos*

[31] Judah Leon Abravanel, "Poem To His Son," trans. Raymond P. Scheindlin

[32] Pedro Calderón de la Barca, *entremés La franchota*, 1672 (a literary portrayal of Gitanos)

[33] Corregidor report from 4 February 1573 on incarcerated Gitanos, Sala de Alcaldes de Casa y Corte, 1609, fols 425 and 434, trans. Richard Pym

[34] Cristóbal Pérez de Herrera, *Amparo de pobres*, 1598 (on the necessity of keeping itinerant groups of Gitanos underfoot), trans. Richard Pym

[35] *Capitulaciones de Granada*, 1492 (the terms of Muslim Granada's surrender to the Christian conquerors), trans. L.P. Harvey

[36] Demófilo (Antonio Machado y Álvarez), *Cantes Flamencos*

I pity them.[37]

The water flows bitter from me[38]
before it can speak its hunger—[39]
we receive nothing:[40]
look how we are lost.[41]

---

[37] Corregidor report from 4 February 1573 on incarcerated Gitanos, trans. Richard Pym

[38] Demófilo (Antonio Machado y Álvarez), *Cantes Flamencos*

[39] Demófilo (Antonio Machado y Álvarez), *Cantes Flamencos*

[40] *Nubdhat al-'asr*, trans. L.P. Harvey

[41] Demófilo (Antonio Machado y Álvarez), *Cantes Flamencos*

III

My soul[42]
whose voice endlessly utters[43]
—oh river!—through the archway,[44]
come near and[45]
know your own beginning:[46]

arise to the harp and the bell, yearn[47]
for the quenching waters,[48]
so composed and untimely [49]
beneath the ground—[50]

[42] Yosef ibn Avitor (Jewish, 940–1024, Mérida, Córdoba, Palestine, North Africa, Egypt), "A Plea," trans. Peter Cole

[43] Yosef ibn Tzaddiq (Jewish, 1070–1149, Córdoba), "Lady of Grace," trans. Peter Cole

[44] José Heredia Maya (Gitano, 1947–2010, Granada), "Por el arco sin fin y sin destino"

[45] Shelomo ibn Gabirol (Jewish, 1021–1058, Málaga, Zaragoza, Granada), "On Leaving Saragossa," trans. Peter Cole

[46] Avraham ibn Ezra (Jewish, 1093–1167, Toledo), "You Whose Hearts Are Asleep," trans. Peter Cole

[47] Yehuda Ha-Levi (Jewish, 1075–1141, Granada, Toledo, Palestine), an *ahava* (love poem), trans. Esperanza Alfonso

[48] Safwan ibn Idris (Muslim, 1165–1202, Murcia), "My Beautiful One," trans. Cola Franzen

[49] "Dónde vas bella judía," letra por peteneras de Rafael Romero 'El Gallina' (Gitano, 1910–1991, Andújar) o de Pastora Pavón Cruz 'La Niña de los Peines' (Gitana, 1890–1969, Sevilla)

[50] Demófilo (Antonio Machado y Álvarez), *Cantes Flamencos*

their successors will ever afterward[51]
appear before us[52]

as juniper stains[53]
fines and penalties,[54]
a lost boat,[55]
scattering pearls,[56]
earth on the tongue, spit,[57]
my body when I left.[58]

You must throw the scraps away—[59]
you should not carry their images.[60]

---

[51] *Capitulaciones de Granada*, 1492, trans. L.P. Harvey

[52] *Charter of the Expulsion of the Jews*, 1492 (document at the behest of King Fernando II of Aragón and Isabel I of Castilla officially announcing the Jews' expulsion from Spain), trans. Edward Peters

[53] Abū l-Hasan 'Ali ibn Hisn (Muslim, eleventh century, Sevilla), "Reflection of Wine," trans. Cola Franzen

[54] Francisco Núñez Muley (Morisco), *A Memorandum for the President of the Royal Audiencia and Chancery Court of the City and Kingdom of Granada*, 1567 (a complaint against a decree meant to crack down on the cultural practices of the Moriscos – that is, nominally converted Muslims living under Christian rule), trans. Vincent Barletta

[55] El Carbonerillo (Gitano, 1906–1937, Sevilla), letra por fandanguillos

[56] Ibn Safr al-Marīnī (Muslim, twelfth century, Almería), "The Valley of Almería," trans. Cola Franzen

[57] José Heredia Maya, "Poema en ritmo menor de 'Sones solo'"

[58] Abūl-Hasan ibn al-Qabturnuh (Muslim, twelfth century, Badajoz), "In The Battle," trans. Cola Franzen

[59] José Heredia Maya, "Los Pulpos"

[60] Ice de Gebir, *Breviario Sunni*, 1462 (instructions/survival guide for Muslims living under Christian rule), trans. L.P. Harvey

They do not cease to pass by,[61]
amphibious and without borders,[62]
though the bells of forgetting sound their alarm:[63]

disordered birdwings in the mouth,[64]
an appointed place
for those who die wanting.[65]

---

[61] Francisco Guanter Espinal 'Paquirri el Guanté' (Gitano, 1834–1862, Cádiz), letra por soleares

[62] José Heredia Maya, "Climatología"

[63] Francisco Guanter Espinal 'Paquirri el Guanté,' letra por soleares

[64] Margalit Matitiahu (Jewish, 1935–, Tel Aviv, writing in Ladino), "Un momento"

[65] Demófilo (Antonio Machado y Álvarez), Cantes Flamencos

Notes

Kol Nidre
Delivered on the eve of Yom Kippur, Kol Nidre is a chant that legally annuls each sinner's broken vows, thereby allowing all members of the congregation to atone before the heavenly court as part of the Jewish community.

Tishrei
Several important Jewish holidays occur during the month of Tishrei —among them is Sukkot, which both commemorates the forty-year biblical journey through the desert and is associated with the harvest. Congregations often celebrate by waving a bouquet made up of date palm, willow, myrtle and citron.

Scenario: Reprise
"Lekabets galuyoteinu" is taken from a section of the Jewish prayer Amdidah. In this particular passage, the congregation asks God to gather and unite exiled Jews.

Tekiah Gedolah
Tekiah gedolah is the long blast of the shofar that is sounded on the Jewish High Holidays.

The Toronto Purchase
The Toronto Purchase was a dubious transaction between the British Crown and the Mississauga Nation in 1787: a treaty in which signatures were transposed onto a blank deed. In the end, the Crown took control of far more land far more permanently than the terms of the

original agreement stipulated, and the ill-acquired territory eventually
became the city called Toronto.

Tikkun olam is the Jewish directive to 'repair the world' by acting
virtuously.

A Cold Series On Sense

Sub/Merge
"La Grande y Felicísima Armada" refers to the Spanish Armada that
was destroyed by storms off the coast of England in 1588.

"nec facundia deseret hunc, nec lucidus ordo.": "neither eloquence
nor lucid order will desert him/this." Horace, *Ars Poetica*, line 41.

Sur/Face
"infelix operis summa, quia ponere totum//nesciet.": "unhappy with
the result, because he is unable to know/create a whole." Horace, *Ars
Poetica*, lines 34-35.

Sub/Rept
"Ordinis haec uirtus erit et uenus": "this will be the virtue and grace
of order/structure," Horace, *Ars Poetica*, line 42.

Sur/Render
"Contra los hombres, no contra los elementos": "against men, not
against the elements." This is a fragment taken from King Philip II
of Spain's reaction to the news that his Armada was destroyed by the
elements rather than by its British foes.

"pleraque differat et praesens in tempus omittat": "[it] disperses and omits a great deal for the present," Horace, *Ars Poetica*, line 44.

Two Months In Granada

Boabdil is the Spanish rendering of Abu Abdallah Muhammad XII (1460-1533), who was the final Muslim ruler of Granada; he was banished from the city by the Christian conquerors in 1492 after surrendering to the forces of Isabel I de Castilla and Fernando II de Aragón.

Mocárabe is a style of ornamentation found on vaults, domes and archways in medieval Islamic architecture.

Para Tocar

"Abre la puerta, niña" is the opening line from the popular band Triana's 1975 song "Abre la Puerta." The band was part of a movement in the 1970s commonly known as 'rock andaluz,' which constituted various sorts of fusion between elements of flamenco and the rock music that the country's youth had absorbed from the anglophone world.

Madinat Garnata was the Arabic name for Muslim Granada before 1492.

Hadar Rimmon

"Rimmon" is Hebrew for "pomegranate," and "Hadar Rimmon" was the name that some Jews used for the city of Granada during the medieval period.

"Sunk in mud, I have dwelt in exile": Solomon ibn Gabirol (Jewish, 1021–1070, Málaga), trans. Dov Jarden/Esperanza Alfonso.

"Rend your mourning garment, and give the Healer what is His": Levi ibn al-Tabban (Jewish, early twelfth century, Zaragoza), trans. Esperanza Alfonso.

"Leave off me now—maybe I'd spend my days in prosperity, a turban above me; I'd drink still water from my well in the cup of deliverance": Samuel ibn Nagrilah (Jewish, 993–1056, Granada), trans. Peter Cole.

After Convivencia
Arise to the harp and the bell, yearn for spiced wine and pomegranate juice. Make the gazelle return to my dwelling": Yehuda ha-Levi (Jewish, 1075–1141, Toledo), trans. Esperanza Alfonso.

"Her glance, like a gazelle's": Ibn Khafaja (Muslim, 1058–1139, Alzira/Valencia, fled to North Africa after the Christian conquest of Valencia), trans. Cola Franzen.

"O dear gazelle! What makes you tarry so?": Judah Leon Abravanel (Jewish, ca.1460–after 1523, Toledo, fled to Italy in 1492 after the Jews were expelled from Spain), trans. Raymond P. Scheindlin.

"Tightly with the cords of my arms lest she escape like a gazelle": Safwan ibn Idris (Muslim, 1164–1202, Murcia), trans. Cola Franzen.

Pellizco
"Pellizco" is the extra tightening, swing, or intensity in a flamenco singer's voice that is often treated as evidence for the ineffable quality known as "duende."

Acknowledgements

My gratitude goes out to many people whose involvement and support has made *Seguiriyas* possible. To name a few: Douglas Kearney and Peter Campion, whose guidance at the University of Minnesota's MFA program ushered this manuscript into its nascent form; Sugi Ganeshananthan, Ray Gonzalez, Sarah Dowling and Kathryn Nuernberger for their helpful feedback on large chunks of the collection; my peers from the MFA program for the sincere energy they put into reading me; Jae Choi, Samiya Bashir, Lisa Steinman, Dustin Simpson and Daniel Khalastchi, for nurturing my writing as it developed; and of course, Carrie Olivia Adams and Janaka Stucky of Black Ocean, for believing in this book. I am, in addition, humbled by the generosity and care that my friends and family have shown me as I've brought these poems into being and grateful for the community that they have given me, in which I continue to dwell, work and learn. Among them are: Khalid Esmail, Brent Bailey, Fan Wu, Ray Osborn, Sarah Schäfer, Vincent Cheng, Megan Gette, Lyes Benarbane, Nico Ramos Flores, Jacqueline Patz DiPiero, David Rodríguez, Alex Algaze, Leslie Hodgkins, Will Harris, Kevin Cicuta, Al Moritz, Ami Xherro, Sean Howard, Will Schmid, James Jones, Mark Saffran, Eli Fox, Loryn Arnett, Matt Prior, Abi Ferstman, David Wang, Nicholas Hassan, Sam West, Julia West, Rebecca Brill, Jesús Leyva Ontiveros, Luigi Sepe Cicala, Juanma Girela, David R. Valeiras, Carmen Peláez Rodríguez, Antonio Molina Flores, Ingrid Ruiz Ruiz and Nacho Gutiérrez Llovio; Raphael Elkabas-Besnard, for two decades of being sure I had this in me; Manuel Heredia Heredia, por los paseos, la música y la afinidad; Isa García Lavandero, for having shared in my joy; Miriam Karraker, Kevin Lee, Anny Chien and Joey McMahon, for offering me an ear when I've needed it most; my grandparents and aunts, Ruth Ross, Sid Ross, Amanda Ross and Karen Grimm, for their staunch encouragement; Sam Meyerson, my brother and closest confidant; Jill Ross and Mark Meyerson, my parents, whose love has always been my first and surest home, no matter how far away I might find myself.

Poems from this book have appeared in the following journals and publications: PANK ("Tekiah Gedolah"); Long Poem Magazine ("Daybreak Translation"); Interim ("Scenario: Entry"); Dusie ("Granada After the Correlation"); Touch The Donkey ("Summer Storm," "Under the Antigua Iglesia de San Miguel in Guadix," and "Living Together"); Periodicities ("Cantabria" and "Para Tocar"); The Alfred Gustav Press (selections from "Months in Granada" formed a micro-chapbook entitled "After Boabdil").